BBC Gardeners' World

POCKET PLANTS

HERBS

Andi Clevely

Photographs by Jo Whitworth

BBC Books

Author Biography

Andi Clevely has been a working gardener for nearly thirty years. He began his career in Leeds City Council central nurseries and since then has worked in many gardens around the country, including Windsor Great Park. He is now responsible for a country estate and large garden in Stratford-on-Avon where he lives with his family. Andi has written a number of gardening books and is a regular columnist for *Homes & Gardens* magazine.

Acknowledgements

The publishers would like to thank Iden Croft Herbs, Staplehurst, Kent; Hollington's Herbs, Newbury, Berkshire; Christina Stapley, East Meon, Hampshire and Secretts Garden Centre, Godalming, Surrey for their assistance with the photography. All photographs © BBC.

Published by BBC Books,
an imprint of BBC Worldwide Publishing.
BBC Worldwide Limited, Woodlands,
80 Wood Lane, London W12 0TT.

First published 1997
© BBC Worldwide Limited 1997
The moral right of the author has been asserted

ISBN 0 563 38779 3

Photographs by Jo Whitworth

Artwork by Pond and Giles

Set in Futura

Printed and bound in Belgium by Proost NV
Colour separations by Radstock Reproductions Limited, Midsomer Norton, Avon
Cover printed in Belgium by Proost NV

Common Names

INTRODUCTION

There is a huge range of plants that can be called herbs. Most of them are attractive garden plants as well as being a home-grown source of fresh flavourings. Herbs are not demanding, and can be added easily to an existing garden. Basic kitchen herbs may be grown near the back door where they are handy, in a small bed or in a collection of pots and other containers. Many are decorative, and can be mixed in with shrubs and flowers in the open garden, while others make neat edgings to paths where they can be harvested in all weathers. Try experimenting with different positions, and remember that the majority are easy to move if a site proves unsuitable.

Growing Conditions

Herbs are not fussy plants on the whole. If you try to think about the natural conditions a particular herb enjoys and position it accordingly, you should have few problems. As a general rule silver, grey and resinous herbs (e.g. rosemary) enjoy full sun and spartan conditions, green leafy herbs (e.g. sorrel) like cool moist shade, and annuals (e.g. parsley, basil) prefer the kind of fertile well-dug soil used for growing vegetables.

The majority dislike waterlogged ground, and good drainage is perhaps the most important precondition – light ground is often the best, while heavy soils can be opened up with plenty of coarse material or gravel. Alternatively, grow them in a raised bed or container where you can provide the conditions they like.

Most herbs thrive in shelter from strong winds, which can injure brittle stems and also destroy that lovely perfumed atmosphere associated with herbs. Hedges of roses and other flowering shrubs can act as protective windbreaks, as will fences supporting climbing plants; dwarf hedges of rosemary, hyssop, santolina and other evergreen herbs help provide shelter, especially when deciduous herbs die down in winter and leave gaps.

Herb types

Annuals: Sown, cropped and cleared all in the same season. Hardy annuals (e.g. chervil) may be sown in spring, or autumn for overwintering; half-hardy or tender annuals (e.g. basil) must be raised under glass for planting out after the last frosts.

Biennials (e.g. evening primrose, parsley): Sown one year to flower and seed the following season; must die down in autumn to a crown or rosette of leaves.

Tender perennials (e.g. lemon verbena, scented pelargoniums): Some herbs from hot climates cannot stand frost and must be protected under glass during winter. It is often best to grow these in pots so that they may be outdoors in summer.

Hardy herbaceous perennials (e.g. mint, tarragon): Live for a number of years, dying down every autumn to a dormant crown that may be out of sight below ground.

Shrubs and shrubby perennials (e.g. bay, thyme): With their woody stems, these plants make permanent bushes, either deciduous or evergreen, and provide interest in winter.

Preparing the soil

Cultivate bare soil, digging the ground as thoroughly as possible, and remove fragments of weed roots as you go: some herbs tend to sprawl as they grow, making surviving weeds difficult to eradicate. If the soil is in good heart, all you need do is fork it over, adding a sprinkling of general fertilizer just before planting. Over larger areas it is possible to prepare the ground and cover it permanently with a sheet of black polythene, planting through holes in this and disguising afterwards with a decorative layer of bark. Before planting, decide where particular herbs are to go – position the tallest at the back of a bed or where they provide shelter, and smaller plants near the front of the bed, together with those used most frequently.

Planting

- Use a spade or trowel to make a hole halt as large again as the plant's roots.

- Position the plant at the same depth as it was growing before.

- Refill the hole around the roots with well-broken soil and firm gently.

- Water thoroughly after planting.

Planting tip – More invasive herbs like mint and tarragon are best kept away from less robust species. Their wandering roots can be confined by planting in containers such as bottomless buckets buried to their rims.

Care

Watering: May be essential in very dry weather and to help young plants become established, but first check the needs of each paricular species. An occasional good soak is more effective than watering little and often.

Feeding: Preparing the ground with some garden compost or mushroom compost (manure is usually too rich) is adequate for most purposes. Many perennials benefit from an annual mulch in autumn or spring, and a light dressing of general fertilizer in spring. Lush leafy crops need more feeding than woody aromatic herbs.

Pruning: This depends on the species. Regular harvesting helps to maintain shape and also encourages bushy growth when growing tips are cut off, but some herbs can be cut down when flowering to extend their usefulness. Most shrubs become old and leggy if not trimmed at least once annually.

Propagation: Some herbs like parsley need sowing every year. Many perennials are short-term plants and either outgrow their position or become old and woody. When this happens you can either buy new plants, or grow your own. Depending on the species there may be self-sown seedlings that can be transplanted, or you can divide herbaceous perennials and replant young portions every few years. Many shrubs can be replaced by layering or taking cuttings every year.

Harvesting: Growing your own herbs allows you to gather a few leaves or tips as needed, but you might also want to harvest large amounts for drying, freezing or some other form of preservation. There is often a best time for this – just before flowering for example – and this is mentioned where appropriate in the text. Some herbs are best dried in sun, others in shade, while a few can be frozen as whole plants or mixed with water in ice-cube trays. Check the best method before harvesting large amounts.

Uses: Over the centuries herbs have been used for a number of purposes, especially culinary and cosmetic, and most are quite safe in moderation. Their medicinal value is more controversial, and mention in this book of their use in various treatments does not amount to recommendation. N.B. Never take unfamiliar herbs as medicines without guidance as even the most benign plant may cause toxic or allergic reactions; diagnosis and prescription should be left to a qualified practitioner or herbalist.

Achillea millefolium Yarrow, Milfoil, Nosebleed

ACHILLEA MILLEFOLIUM

A familiar lawn weed but also a classical herb said to have been used by Achilles to heal the wounds of war. The young ferny leaves are peppery and used sparingly in salads, while the small white daisies dry well for winter decoration.

Plant type:	Hardy perennial.
Season of use:	Pick leaves to use fresh in spring and summer; cut just before flowering for drying. Cut flowers summer and autumn.
Height:	15–60cm (6–24in)
Spread:	45cm (18in)
Soil:	Well-drained; good for chalk and dry sites.
Positioning:	Full sun or light shade, 30cm (12in) apart.
Planting time:	Spring or autumn.
Propagation:	Sow seeds early spring; divide plants spring or autumn.
Care:	Roots spread readily, so segregate from less robust plants. Cut down in autumn.
Recommended:	Basic species for herbal use; 'Summer Pastels', 'Cerise Queen' for flowers.
Related plants:	*A. decolorans* (English Mace), slightly tender perennial with yellow flowers; *A. moschata* (Musk Yarrow), dwarf with white flowers in summer.

Agastache foeniculum
Anise Hyssop, Giant Hyssop

❋❋

Plant type: Hardy (short-lived) perennial.

Season of use: Use fresh all summer; gather for drying just before or during flowering.

Height: 90cm (3ft)

Spread: 45–60cm (18–24in)

Soil: Light, rich and free-draining.

Positioning: Full sun or very light shade, 45cm (18in) apart, with shelter from cold winds.

Planting time: Mid- to late spring.

Propagation: Sow early summer under glass; take semi-ripe cuttings in summer and overwinter in a cold frame; divide the plant in spring.

Care: Mulch spring and autumn on dry soils, and feed every spring. In cold gardens, pot up and overwinter in a cold frame. Take cuttings in summer as an insurance, and renew plants every 3–4 years.

Recommended: Basic species; also white forms 'Alba' and 'Alabaster.'

Related plants: A. mexicana (Mexican Hyssop, Mexican Bergamot), scarlet or crimson flowers.

AGASTACHE FOENICULUM

A North American relative of bergamot, with neat clumps of aromatic foliage and from mid-summer onwards fragrant terminal spikes of flowers that are popular with bees. The aniseed-flavoured leaves can be used fresh or dried for flavouring and for making teas. (syn. A. anethiodora, A. anisata.)

Aloysia triphylla Lemon Verbena, Herb Luisa

ALOYSIA TRIPHYLLA

As a native of South America, this deliciously scented herb is best grown as a pot plant in cold gardens. The leaves have a strong lemon flavour, and when dried keep their fragrance for many months. It is widely used for medicinal preparations. The young shoots are distilled for essential oil. (syn. *Lippia citriodora*.)

Plant type:	Slightly tender perennial.
Season of use:	Pick leaves at any time to use fresh, or dry in shade.
Height:	1.5m (5ft), more in warm climates.
Spread:	1–1.5m (3–5ft)
Soil:	Fertile, well-drained and slightly alkaline.
Positioning:	Full sun with shelter from cold winds, preferably at the foot of a sunny wall, as a pot plant indoors or in a greenhouse border.
Planting time:	After last spring frosts.
Propagation:	Sow in spring under glass; take soft cuttings in early summer.
Care:	Mulch spring and autumn, and feed in spring. Prune annually to shape, and propagate every few years from cuttings as older plants are less tolerant of cold. Prune pot plants in spring and stand outdoors after frosts; rehouse in autumn and keep almost dry.
Recommended:	Basic species only available.
Related plants:	*Lippia dulcis* (Aztec Sweet Herb), intensely sweet.

Plant type: Hardy perennial bulb.
Season of use: Spring to autumn; also winter in pots indoors.
Height: 23cm (9in)
Spread: 10–15cm (4–6in)
Soil: Rich and well-drained, with plenty of humus.
Positioning: 23cm (9in) apart in rows, in full sun or light shade.
Planting time: Mid-spring.
Propagation: Sow in spring, outdoors in rows or in seed trays under glass; divide mature clumps every 3–5 years in spring or autumn.
Care: Keep moist during growth. Cut back once or twice during summer. Pot up divisions in autumn and keep in a cold frame until required indoors.
Recommended: Only basic species available, sometimes as larger-leaved selections.
Related plants: A. tuberosum (Chinese Chives, Garlic Chives), larger with mild garlic flavour; A. fistulosum (Welsh Onions, Bunching Onions), evergreen leaves and strong flavour.

ALLIUM SCHOENOPRASUM

An essential kitchen herb, forming neat hummocks of fine, bright green leaves that withstand frequent cutting. The clusters of subtly flavoured mauve or purple flowers are also edible. Popular as an edging plant and for attracting bees.

Anethum graveolens Dill, Dillweed

ANETHUM GRAVEOLENS

The soft, blue-green filigree leaves and small creamy-yellow flowers make this an attractive herb for growing as a crop in the kitchen garden. It is widely used as a condiment and flavouring in North European cooking, and as an aid to digestion in 'dill water'.

Plant type: Tender annual.

Season of use: Pick leaves and flowers throughout growing season to use fresh; dry seeds for winter use.

Height: 45–75cm (18–30in)

Spread: 45cm (18in)

Soil: Fertile, light and free-draining.

Positioning: Full sun, in rows 60cm (24in) apart or in patches; thin to small groups 30cm (12in) apart.

Planting time: Always sown in situ in spring and autumn.

Propagation: Sow outdoors in spring and again in early summer.

Care: Water regularly during growth. Pick seedheads before fully mature and spread on trays to dry.

Recommended: Species only available; distinct strains for leaf or seed production.

Related plants: A. 'Sowa' (Indian Dill), more pungent, used in Asian cooking.

Angelica archangelica Garden Angelica

Plant type: Hardy biennial or (short-lived) perennial.

Season of use: Pick leaves to use fresh during growing season; cut stems in summer of second year and gather seedheads in late summer; dig roots just before flowering.

Height: 1.8m (6ft)

Spread: 75cm (30in)

Soil: Cool, moist and full of humus.

Positioning: Partial shade, in woodland or at the back of herb and flower borders.

Planting time: Spring or autumn.

Propagation: Sow in situ in autumn, or pre-chill seeds in a refrigerator for a few weeks before sowing indoors in spring. Take offsets in spring or autumn from the base of mature plants.

Care: Keep moist at all times. Cut down stems in autumn, mulch generously, and feed in spring.

Recommended: Species only available.

Related plants: *A. atropurpurea* (Purple Angelica), rounded leaves, medicinal uses; *A. gigas* (Korean Angelica), purple flowers.

ANGELICA ARCHANGELICA

A stout plant, used medicinally, for flavouring and as a candied sweet or cake decoration; the stems can even be cooked like rhubarb. Plants seed freely, but transplant seedlings while still very young, because the roots are strong and tenacious.

Anthriscus cerefolium
Salad Chervil, Garden Chervil

ANTHRISCUS CEREFOLIUM

A pretty annual, spread throughout Europe by the Romans and one of the most important French culinary herbs, sweet and slightly aniseed-flavoured. Plants are slender and best grown in patches, leaving some to seed and create a permanent bed.

Plant type:	Hardy annual.
Season of use:	Pick leaves to use fresh from spring to autumn; for freezing or drying gather leaves just before flowering.
Height:	45cm (18in)
Spread:	30cm (12in)
Soil:	Light and moist, but not waterlogged.
Positioning:	Full sun or light shade, in wide rows or patches; late summer seedlings in pots on a warm windowsill over winter.
Planting time:	Always sown in situ in spring and summer.
Propagation:	Sow in situ 3–4 times in spring and summer, and again in late summer for overwintering.
Care:	Little attention needed, apart from watering in dry weather. Gather leaves and shoot-tips frequently to delay flowering.
Recommended:	Basic species only available.
Related plants:	Many similar plants in the cow parsley family, some of them poisonous, so do not gather chervil from the wild.

Armoracia rusticana Horseradish

Plant type: Hardy perennial.

Season of use: Pick young leaves in spring and cook as spinach; dig roots any time, or harvest in autumn and store.

Height: 75cm (30in)

Spread: 30cm (12in)

Soil: Moist, rich and fortified with humus.

Positioning: Full sun or light shade, 30cm (12in) apart.

Planting time: Early spring.

Propagation: Take root cuttings 15cm (6in) long in early spring; sow seeds in spring (basic species only).

Care: Water well in dry weather. Dig up all roots in autumn and store in moist sand.

Recommended: Basic species widely available; 'Variegata' has attractive white leaf markings.

Related plants: None.

ARMORACIA RUSTICANA

A familiar condiment and medicinal herb, and one of the most tenacious plants: any overlooked root fragment will survive to colonize neglected corners. The best roots come from annual crops, lifted wholesale in autumn for storing and replanted the next spring.

13

Arnica chamissonis Arnica, Leopards Bane

ARNICA CHAMISSONIS

For centuries the herbalist's traditional source of arnicine for treating bruises was *A. montana*, now endangered in the wild and hard to grow. *A. chamissonis* is the modern substitute offered by most nurseries (toxic if taken internally).

Plant type:	Hardy perennial.
Season of use:	Pick leaves to use fresh at any time; cut flower heads to dry in late summer.
Height:	90cm (3ft)
Spread:	30–45cm (12–18in)
Soil:	Moist and rich in humus, slightly acid.
Positioning:	Full sun or semi-shade, 30cm (12in) apart.
Planting time:	Spring or autumn.
Propagation:	Sow in spring in a cold frame (germination often slow); divide rosettes of leaves in autumn.
Care:	Cut down top growth in autumn and mulch with compost. Feed at half-strength in spring.
Recommended:	Only basic species available.
Related plants:	*A. montana* (Arnica, Mountain Tobacco), smaller plant with yellow flowers, very poisonous.

Artemisia dracunculus French Tarragon, Estragon

Plant type: Herbaceous perennial.
Season of use: Cut growing tips in spring and summer; top growth can be harvested at flowering time for slow drying.
Height: 60cm (2ft)
Spread: 30cm (12in) or more
Soil: Rich and well-drained (cannot tolerate wet ground).
Positioning: Warm sunny borders, 23cm (9in) apart.
Planting time: Mid-spring or autumn on light soil.
Propagation: Take soft cuttings in early summer; divide roots in spring or autumn.
Care: Keep weed-free during growth, water in dry weather, and protect roots with a mulch of compost. Propagate every 3–4 years, replanting in fresh soil.
Recommended: Only basic species available.
Related plants: *A. dracunculoides* (Russian Tarragon), more vigorous, 90cm (3ft) or more, inferior flavour; *A. abrotanum* (Southernwood), aromatic woody shrub; *A. absinthium* (Wormwood), bitter perennial shrub.

ARTEMISIA DRACUNCULUS

A slim creeping perennial, with smooth, pale green aromatic leaves that have been used medicinally since Roman times, although now it is best known as a culinary herb and an essential ingredient in French cooking.

Atriplex hortensis Orach, Mountain Spinach

ATRIPLEX HORTENSIS

Although both green and red forms have been cultivated for centuries as a herb and leaf vegetable, orach is now more often seen in flower gardens. It is still used widely in soups and salads in France, sometimes added to sorrel to reduce the latter's acidity.

Plant type:	Hardy annual.
Season of use:	Gather the leaves at any time during the growing season.
Height:	Up to 2.4m (8ft)
Spread:	75cm (30in)
Soil:	Any ordinary and fairly fertile well-drained soil.
Positioning:	Full sun, 45–60cm (18–24in) apart in groups in a herb or kitchen garden, or as decorative plants in flower beds.
Planting time:	Normally sown in situ; transplant seedlings in late spring.
Propagation:	Sow seeds in early spring, outdoors where plants are to grow or, if preferred, in pots for transplanting as soon as large enough.
Care:	Undemanding. If plants show signs of running to seed, sow a further batch for late use. Plants self-seed freely
Recommended:	Basic green species; purple-red var. *rubra* (syn. var. *atrosanguinea*) is popular as an ornamental plant.
Related plants:	None.

Borago officinalis Borage, Bee Bread

Plant type: Hardy biennial, often grown as an annual.

Season of use: Use young spring leaves in salads. Summer flowers used fresh, candied or dried; whole flowering plant dried in summer for medicinal use.

Height: 60–75cm (24–30in)

Spread: 30cm (12in)

Soil: Light and free-draining but not impoverished.

Positioning: Full sun or very light shade, 23cm (9in) apart.

Planting time: Plant seedlings in late spring.

Propagation: Sow in situ in spring for summer use, and again in late summer to overwinter seedlings. Plants often self-seed freely.

Care: Little attention needed; leave some plants to self-seed and then thin seedlings the following spring.

Recommended: Blue species normally available

Related plants: B. o. 'Alba', good white form; B. laxiflora, syn. B. pygmaea (Corsican Borage), coarse perennial with paler flowers, thriving in poor stony soil.

BORAGO OFFICINALIS

One of the best blue flowers of any kind, borage is as much at home in an ornamental border as in the herb garden, where it is grown as a popular bee plant and for its large flowers that are used to garnish summer drinks and salads.

Calamintha grandiflora Large Calamint

CALAMINTHA GRANDIFLORA

Formerly a member of the Savory genus, this is a strongly aromatic herb with peppermint-flavoured leaves that are infused to make a pleasant tea. It was widely used medicinally in the Middle Ages but is now grown mainly as an ornamental.

Plant type:	Hardy perennial.
Season of use:	Pick leaves to use fresh in summer; harvest leaves or whole plant just before flowering for drying.
Height:	30–45cm (12–18in)
Spread:	30cm (12in)
Soil:	Light, with plenty of humus and slightly alkaline.
Positioning:	Dappled shade, 30cm (12in) apart.
Planting time:	Mid-spring.
Propagation:	Sow early to mid-spring in situ; take cuttings of side-shoots in spring; divide roots autumn or late spring.
Care:	Mulch in spring and top dress with general fertilizer. Cut down all growth in autumn.
Recommended:	Basic species normally available; also 'Variegata' with cream leaf markings.
Related plants:	*C. nepeta* (Lesser Calamint), bushy aromatic perennial 30cm (12in) high, white or lilac flowers; *C. sylvatica* ssp. *ascendens* (Common Calamint), very similar to *C. grandiflora*, mauve flowers.

Calendula officinalis Pot Marigold, English Marigold

Plant type:	Hardy annual, biennial or short-lived perennial.
Season of use:	Pick leaves and flowers to use fresh in spring and summer.
Height:	30–45cm (12–18in)
Spread:	30cm (12in)
Soil:	Best in heavier soils, free-draining with low fertility.
Positioning:	Full sun or light shade in patches, combined with purple or bronze herbs for dramatic effect.
Planting time:	Normally sown in situ in spring.
Propagation:	Sow in spring for late summer, or in autumn for earlier and longer flowering the following year.
Care:	Thin to 10–15cm (4–6in) apart. Deadhead regularly to prolong flowering, but leave some plants to self-seed.
Recommended:	'Orange King', 'Radio'; also coloured double forms such as 'Fiesta Gitana' and 'Art Shades'. C. o. 'Prolifera' (Hen and Chicks Marigold), flowers ringed with smaller blooms.
Related plants:	None.

CALENDULA OFFICINALIS

A familiar and atmospheric cottage garden flower, especially in its basic bright orange form. The edible blooms have been used as a yellow food colourant as well as a medicinal herb since earliest Greek and Arabic times.

19

Carum carvi Caraway

CARUM CARVI

Although best known for its seeds, which were used as far back as prehistoric times both for flavouring and an aid to digestion, caraway is also cultivated as an alternative root crop to parsnips, as a potent medicinal plant and for flavouring liqueurs such as kümmel.

Plant type:	Hardy biennial, sometimes treated as an annual.
Season of use:	Pick young leaves to use fresh in first summer; dig roots in winter; gather seeds late in second summer.
Height:	60cm (24in) second year
Spread:	20cm (8in)
Soil:	Light and well-drained for seed crops, moist and fertile for roots.
Positioning:	Full sun, in rows 20cm (8in) apart.
Planting time:	Sow in spring and summer, in situ only as it cannot be transplanted.
Propagation:	Sow in situ mid- to late summer for seed crops, or early spring for roots.
Care:	Thin to 15cm (6in) apart. In their first year plants produce rosettes of feathery leaves, which should be left intact unless needed for their roots. Late the second summer cut seedheads before fully ripe and dry indoors for shelling.
Recommended:	Only the species normally available.
Related plants:	None.

Plant type:	Hardy perennial.
Season of use:	Use non-flowering forms all year for lawns and herbal seats; cut flowers in summer, fresh and for drying.
Height:	25cm (10in)
Spread:	30cm (12in)
Soil:	Light, fertile and free-draining, slightly acid.
Positioning:	Full sun, 30cm (12in) apart for specimens, 15cm (6in) for lawns.
Planting time:	Late spring.
Propagation:	Sow in spring outdoors or under cool glass (do not cover seeds); divide plants in spring.
Care:	Water in dry weather. Camomile lawns need careful weeding and a balanced feed each spring. Divide and renew plants every 3–4 years.
Recommended:	'Flore Pleno' (double-flowered) for specimen plants; non-flowering 'Treneague' for lawns.
Related plants:	*Anthemis tinctoria* (Dyer's Chamomile), perennial with yellow flowers; *Matricaria recutita* (German Chamomile), annual up to 60cm (2ft) tall, white/yellow flowers.

CHAMAEMELUM NOBILE

Camomile tea is almost as well known as the camomile lawns and seats of Elizabethan gardens. The fresh apple fragrance of the flowers and foliage is stimulating, and plants have been an ingredient in cosmetics since Egyptian times. (syn. *Anthemis nobilis.*)

Chenopodium bonus-henricus Good King Henry, Mercury

CHENOPODIUM BONUS-HENRICUS

This prehistoric leaf and seed vegetable is now generally regarded as a herb, regionally popular for its fleshy and nutritious leaves. The young shoots are sometimes earthed up and blanched as an alternative to true asparagus.

Plant type:	Hardy herbaceous perennial.
Season of use:	Pick young leaves and shoots in early spring.
Height:	75cm (30in)
Spread:	60cm (2ft)
Soil:	Light, free-draining and very fertile.
Positioning:	Light shade best, 45cm (18in) apart.
Planting time:	Spring or autumn.
Propagation:	Sow in spring in situ or in a nursery bed; divide plants in spring.
Care:	Water well in dry weather, feed each spring or mulch with rotted manure in autumn. Plants self-seed readily, so remove flower heads as they form.
Recommended:	Basic species only.
Related plants:	C. quinoa (Quinoa), South American annual, seeds used as a well-known cereal.

Cichorium intybus Chicory, Succory

Plant type:	Hardy herbaceous perennial.
Season of use:	Cut flowers fresh in summer; dig roots in autumn for drying or forcing.
Height:	1.5m (5ft)
Spread:	45cm (18in)
Soil:	Rich, free-draining and slightly alkaline.
Positioning:	Full sun, 20–30cm (8–12in) apart.
Planting time:	Sow in situ in spring, but spare roots may be transplanted with care in autumn.
Propagation:	Sow seeds in situ early in spring.
Care:	Thin to final spacings; mulch as plants grow, water in dry weather and feed once or twice for root crops. Cut down ornamental plants and dig roots in autumn; trim and store in sand, and force in warmth and darkness.
Recommended:	Basic species for flowering plants; 'Witloof', 'Apollo' for forcing chicons; basic species or 'Witloof' for a coffee substitute.
Related plants:	Numerous other forms of chicory, radicchio and endive grown for salads.

CICHORIUM INTYBUS

The clear electric blue of the flowers is a stunning sight, especially in the early morning sunlight. The thick deep taproots are widely used medicinally, or roasted and ground as a coffee substitute. They are also forced in order to develop young shoots (chicons) for winter salads.

Coriandrum sativum Coriander

CORIANDRUM SATIVUM 'SANTO'

An important herb with the simple grace of a wild flower. Its roots and leaves, an acquired taste for some people, are widely used in Asian cooking, while the deliciously aromatic seeds are a well-known condiment.

Plant type:	Hardy annual (may be injured in cold winters).
Season of use:	Pick young leaves and shoots any time; dig roots after flowering; gather ripe seeds in autumn.
Height:	60cm (2ft)
Spread:	30–45cm (12–18in)
Soil:	Light and well-drained, with a little lime.
Positioning:	Full sun, in rows 20cm (8in) apart; shelter the brittle stems from strong winds.
Planting time:	Always sown in situ, spring to autumn.
Propagation:	Sow seeds in spring, and again in late summer or early autumn.
Care:	Thin to 15cm (6in) apart. The best plants are grown fast, so top-dress the soil with general fertilizer before sowing and water regularly in dry weather. Harvest before seeds are shed.
Recommended:	Basic species for seed production; 'Cilantro' for leaf crops.
Related plants:	*Nigella sativa* (Roman Coriander, Black Cumin), aromatic seeds used for seasoning.

Dianthus gratianopolitanus Cheddar Pink

Plant type: Hardy evergreen perennial.

Season of use: Gather the flowers in summer and use fresh as flavouring, or dry for pot-pourri.

Height: 20cm (8in)

Spread: 20cm (8in)

Soil: Light and well-drained, with a little lime.

Positioning: Full sun, 15cm (6in) apart in small groups and as edging or ground cover.

Planting time: Spring.

Propagation: Sow seeds in autumn or spring in a cold frame; strike cuttings, pulled off with a heel, in early autumn in a cold frame or outdoors.

Care: General fertilizer in spring. Deadhead and lightly trim to shape after flowering. Take cuttings and renew straggly plants after 3–4 years.

Recommended: Basic species. 'Albus' (white); 'Flore Pleno' (double); 'Splendens' (large flowers).

Related plants: *D. caryophyllus* (Clove Pink or Border Carnation), *D. deltoides* (Maiden Pink), *D. plumarius* (Pink).

DIANTHUS GRATIANOPOLITANUS

Only the flowers have herbal uses, as flavouring for drinks and for decorating food or pot-pourri, but pinks of all kinds have always been regarded as classic herb garden flowers, planted liberally for their life-enhancing colours and fragrance.

Dictamnus albus
Burning Bush, White Dittany

DICTAMNUS ALBUS

An ornamental herb with pungent leaves used to make a medicinal tea. In a hot summer the flowers exude volatile oils that can be ignited briefly with a match (this may happen spontaneously). Despite its name, flowers may be pink or light purple. (syn. *Dictamnus fraxinella albus*.)

Plant type:	Hardy herbaceous perennial.
Season of use:	Cut flowers in early summer, to use fresh or dried; pick leaves in summer for culinary and medicinal use.
Height:	60–75cm (24–30in)
Spread:	30cm (12in)
Soil:	Preferably light and dry; not heavy clay.
Positioning:	Full sun or light shade, 30cm (12in) apart, with shelter from strong winds.
Planting time:	Autumn; spring (plants may not flower until following year).
Propagation:	Sow outdoors in late summer or early autumn; take root cuttings early spring; divide plants autumn or spring.
Care:	Little necessary. Feed established plants in spring and mulch with compost or leaves in autumn; deadhead after flowering. Divide plants every 4–5 years.
Recommended:	Basic species; also var. *purpureus* (pink, red-veined flowers).
Related plants:	None.

Eruca vesicaria (Salad) Rocket, Roquette

❋❋

Plant type:	Hardy annual.
Season of use:	Pick leaves and flowers to use fresh in summer and autumn, or all year round in warm districts or with protection.
Height:	60cm (2ft)
Spread:	30cm (12in)
Soil:	Rich and moist, slightly alkaline.
Positioning:	Full sun, or light shade for summer crops on dry soils.
Planting time:	Usually sown in situ in spring and summer.
Propagation:	Sow in spring and mid- to late summer.
Care:	Thin to 23cm (9in) apart each way. Spring-sown plants run quickly to seed in drought, so water consistently. Cover late sowings in autumn for protection.
Recommended:	Basic species; sometimes cultivated selections available.
Related plants:	None.

ERUCA VESICARIA

Grown for centuries as a cottage garden plant, rocket has been revived as a pungent addition to Mediterranean salads. Both flowers and leaves are used, while the fat crisp seedpods are edible and medicinal, and also a source of mustard oils. (syn. *E. sativa*.)

Filipendula ulmaria Meadowsweet

FILIPENDULA ULMARIA

An exceptionally pretty and fragrant wild flower, used in medieval times as a strewing herb and for pain relief (an early source of aspirin). A stately plant that needs plenty of space in a herbaceous border or at the back of the herb garden.

Plant type:	Hardy herbaceous perennial.
Season of use:	Harvest young leaves and shoots in early summer; cut flowers fresh in summer or use dried.
Height:	1.2m (4ft)
Spread:	60cm (2ft)
Soil:	Moist, fertile and slightly alkaline.
Positioning:	Full sun or semi-shade.
Planting time:	Autumn.
Propagation:	Sow in spring, in situ or in trays under cool glass; divide plants in autumn.
Care:	Water generously in dry weather, mulch with compost in spring and autumn, and feed each spring. Deadhead after flowering and cut down top growth in autumn.
Recommended:	Basic species for herbal use; gold-leafed 'Aurea', pink 'Rosea' and double 'Flore Pleno' for flowers.
Related plants:	*F. vulgaris*, syn. *F. hexapetala* (Dropwort), smaller plant, with attractive double form 'Multiplex'.

Plant type:	Hardy herbaceous perennial.
Season of use:	Harvest growing tips and young leaves in spring and early summer; gather seeds in autumn and dry in warmth.
Height:	2m (6ft)
Spread:	60cm (2ft)
Soil:	Light and moist, free-draining and fertile.
Positioning:	Full sun or light shade, 45cm (18in) apart, sheltered from winds.
Planting time:	Spring and summer.
Propagation:	Sow in spring, in situ or in small pots under cool glass; divide plants in spring.
Care:	Plants have strong taproots so transplant at less than 1 year old. Mulch in autumn and feed in spring; for prolonged harvest, water well in dry weather. Deadhead after flowering unless grown as a seed crop. Divide and renew every 3–4 years.
Recommended:	Basic species, or a coloured variant such as 'Giant Bronze', 'Purpureum', 'Smokey'.
Related plants:	F. v. 'Dulce' (Florence Fennel, Sweet Fennel).

FOENICULUM VULGARE 'PURPUREUM'

An indispensable culinary and medicinal herb since ancient times, still widely valued for its aniseed flavour and digestive virtues. It is handsome and versatile, useful for leaf and seed crops, and also as an ornamental, especially combined with bergamot.

Fragaria vesca Wild Strawberry, Wood strawberry

FRAGARIA VESCA

Plant type:	Hardy herbaceous perennial.
Season of use:	Gather ripe fruits in summer; pick leaves to use fresh spring to autumn; dry leaves for winter use; dig roots in winter.
Height:	25cm (10in)
Spread:	25cm (10in)
Soil:	All moist, fertile soils except heavy clay.
Positioning:	Light shade, 23cm (9in) apart.
Planting time:	Spring or autumn.
Propagation:	Surface-sow in autumn under cool glass; plantlets ('runners') transplant in spring or autumn.
Care:	Water in dry weather, mulch in spring and autumn and feed each spring. Trim off old foliage after cropping and remove surplus runners.
Recommended:	True wild species best; also 'Mara des Bois', 'Rügen' and 'Variegata', and white 'Fructu Albo'.
Related plants:	*F. virginiana* (Scarlet Strawberry), North American medicinal plant and parent of large-fruited forms.

Birds seldom plunder the sweetly flavoured fruits in the same way as they do larger cultivated forms. Plants are also used for herbal purposes, the leaves as an ingredient in salads or medicinal teas, and all parts including the roots to make iron tonics.

Galega officinalis Goat's Rue

Plant type: Hardy herbaceous perennial.

Season of use: Gather fresh leaves any time during the growing season; the whole flowering plant may be cut for drying; dry seeds in autumn for medicinal use.

Height: Up to 1.5m (5ft)

Spread: 60cm (2ft)

Soil: Rich, fertile and moist.

Positioning: Full sun, in a herb border or wild garden, as single specimens or 45cm (18in) apart in groups of 3–4 plants.

Planting time: Autumn or spring.

Propagation: Sow seeds in spring in a cold frame; divide plants in autumn or spring.

Care: Mulch and feed with a general fertilizer in spring. Water in hot dry seasons. Cut down top growth in autumn.

Recommended: Basic species, and white form 'Alba'; 'His Majesty' (white and pink) and 'Lady Wilson' (mauve) are good selections for the flower garden.

Related plants: None.

GALEGA OFFICINALIS

Large bushy plants and the long racemes of blooms that appear from mid-summer onwards guarantee a place for goat's rue in the flower border, but its reputation was made as a milk stimulant for nursing mothers. The juice is also used to clot milk for cheese-making.

Galium odoratum Sweet Woodruff

GALIUM ODORATUM

An old strewing herb and a lovely creeping plant for shady places. Plants cut at flowering time and hung up to dry release the heady and pervasive sweet perfume of newly mown hay. Widely used for medicinal purposes and to make refreshing teas. (syn. *Asperula odorata*.)

Plant type:	Hardy herbaceous perennial.
Season of use:	Pick leaves to use fresh, spring to late summer. Cut whole plant at or just before flowering in early summer and dry slowly.
Height:	30–38cm (12–15in)
Spread:	30cm (12in)
Soil:	Rich, moist and leafy, slightly alkaline.
Positioning:	Shade or semi-shade.
Planting time:	Any time.
Propagation:	Sow in situ or in seed trays, in late summer and expose to frost; divide roots at any time.
Care:	Undemanding. A spring mulch helps to keep soils moist; cut down top growth in autumn. Harvest from the second year.
Recommended:	Basic species only.
Related plants:	*G. verum* (Lady's Bedstraw), taller, with scented flowers once used to colour cheese; stems give a red dye.

Genista tinctoria Dyer's Greenweed, Dyer's Broom

Plant type: Hardy deciduous dwarf shrub.

Season of use: Pick young flowering shoots in early summer, to use fresh or for drying; cut flower buds and flowers in summer.

Height: 1.2m (4ft)

Spread: 75cm (30in)

Soil: Light, free-draining and slightly alkaline, not too fertile.

Positioning: Full sun, 60cm (24in) apart.

Planting time: Spring or autumn.

Propagation: Sow seeds (first rubbed between sheets of sandpaper) outdoors in situ or in a nursery bed; graft named cultivars on laburnum rootstocks in spring.

Care: Mulch in spring. Prune lightly after flowering, and again in spring to remove winter die-back and to shape plants.

Recommended: Basic species; 'Flore Pleno' (double) and 'Royal Gold' (brighter colour and more flowers).

Related plants: Many other genistas grown in gardens, but with ornamental use only.

GENISTA TINCTORIA 'ROYAL GOLD'

A dye plant, its flowers produce a rich yellow or green according to the process used. The flowering shoots are used medicinally, while flower buds can be pickled like capers. Cultivated forms are smaller and longer flowering than the species.

Glycyrrhiza glabra Liquorice, Licorice

GLYCYRRHIZA GLABRA

An historic and atmospheric plant for herb collections, reminiscent of childhood days. Commercial liquorice is made from lavishly cultivated roots, but plants are also quietly decorative with attractive flowers from mid- to late summer and long brown seedpods.

❋❋

Plant type:	Hardy herbaceous perennial.
Season of use:	Dig roots in autumn or spring for drying.
Height:	1.5m (5ft)
Spread:	75cm (30in)
Soil:	Deep, fertile and well-drained.
Positioning:	Full sun, 10cm (4in) deep and 45cm (18in) apart.
Planting time:	Autumn or spring.
Propagation:	Divide roots at harvest time.
Care:	Undemanding; the best roots need high fertility, with annual spring feeds and a thick mulch in autumn for winter protection. Cut down growth in autumn, remove creeping runners, and harvest when 3–4 years old.
Recommended:	Basic species; improved selections occasionally available.
Related plants:	None.

Hamamelis virginiana Witch Hazel

❄❄

Plant type:	Hardy deciduous shrub or small tree.
Season of use:	Harvest flowering shoots and bark in late autumn for distillation; cut ornamental sprigs autumn and winter.
Height:	5m (15ft)
Spread:	5m (15ft)
Soil:	Moist and slightly acid.
Positioning:	Full or light shade, with shelter from cold winds.
Planting time:	Autumn or spring.
Propagation:	Sow in autumn in pots or trays and expose to frost; take cuttings from stems bearing aerial roots; root suckers in autumn.
Care:	Water in dry weather and feed each spring with rose fertilizer; mulch autumn and late spring. Straggly stems may be shortened or removed in spring. Cut, mow or transplant suckers.
Recommended:	Basic species; also many ornamental garden forms.
Related plants:	*H. mollis* (Chinese Witch Hazel), ornamental shrub with many handsome cultivars but no herbal associations.

HAMAMELIS VIRGINIANA

This is the source of the familiar astringent skin medication. It is an appealing tree, with bright yellow autumn tints and an attractive spreading habit if allowed to reach full height. The flowers are not as sweetly scented as in other species.

Helichrysum italicum Curry Plant

HELICHRYSUM ITALICUM

Highly aromatic shrub with a spicy curry fragrance, an ornamental shrub as well as a valuable herb for culinary and cosmetic uses. Some consider the flowers detract from the intense silvery-white foliage, but they are useful for flower arranging. (syn. *H. angustifolium*.)

Plant type:	Moderately hardy evergreen shrub.
Season of use:	Pick leaves to use fresh at any time; pick flower buds in summer for dried arrangements; pick flower heads and shoots in summer for distillation.
Height:	60cm (2ft)
Spread:	30cm (12in)
Soil:	Light and free-draining, with moderate fertility.
Positioning:	Full sun, protected from frosts and cold winds in winter. Makes an excellent low hedge.
Planting time:	Autumn or spring.
Propagation:	Sow in trays under cool glass in spring; take soft cuttings in summer.
Care:	Mulch in spring and feed with rose fertilizer. In formal positions trim off flowering stems as they appear; trim in spring but never cut back into old wood. Screen plants in very severe winters.
Recommended:	Basic species; also *H. i.* ssp. *microphyllum* and 'Nanum', both dwarf forms.
Related plants:	*H. stoechas* (Goldilocks), dwarf, best form 'White Barn'.

Humulus lupulus Hop(s)

Plant type: Perennial herbaceous climber.

Season of use: Pick young shoots in spring; gather female cones in early autumn for drying.

Height: Up to 4.5m (15ft)

Spread: 2m (6ft)

Soil: Rich, moist, with plenty of humus.

Positioning: Full sun or light shade, sheltered from cold winds.

Planting time: Late winter or early spring.

Propagation: Take semi-ripe cuttings in late summer and grow on in heat; divide roots in spring.

Care: Mulch in autumn with well-rotted manure and feed in spring. Thin young shoots to 5–6 per crown and water freely in dry weather. Gather cones while still green and hang up to dry until brown. Cut growth back to soil level in late autumn.

Recommended: 'Aureus' is the normal golden hop; also basic species in large gardens.

Related plants: None.

HUMULUS LUPULUS 'AUREUS'

Decorative and less vigorous than the plain form, and best grown on a screen or festooned on ropes between poles. Surplus young shoots can be harvested like asparagus in spring, while the familiar cones are a herbal sedative.

Hyssopus officinalis Hyssop

HYSSOPUS OFFICINALIS

Charming and decorative as a specimen or low hedge, and renowned for its medicinal and culinary uses. The distilled oil is an ingredient in perfumes and liqueurs. It is typically blue-flowered, but equally desirable in other colour forms.

Plant type: Hardy perennial shrub.

Season of use: Pick leaves to use fresh at any time; pick flowering tips in late summer, fresh or for drying.

Height: 60cm (2ft)

Spread: 30cm (12in)

Soil: Light, well-drained and slightly alkaline.

Positioning: Full sun for compact growth, 20cm (8in) apart for a dwarf hedge.

Planting time: Early to late spring.

Propagation: Sow in spring under glass; take semi-ripe cuttings in early summer; divide plants spring or autumn.

Care: Mulch in autumn and feed with a rose fertilizer in spring. Trim lightly in autumn to reduce wind resistance, and again in spring to maintain shape.

Recommended: Basic species; also 'Albus' (white), 'Purpurascens' (red) and 'Roseus' (pink).

Related plants: *Agastache foeniculum* (Anise Hyssop), aromatic herbaceous perennial.

Plant type: Hardy herbaceous perennial.

Season of use: Pick leaves in spring and summer, to use fresh or for drying; dig 2-year-old roots in autumn for shredding and drying.

Height: Up to 2.5m (8ft)

Spread: 60cm (2ft)

Soil: Moist and fertile.

Positioning: Light shade or full sun.

Planting time: Autumn or spring.

Propagation: Sow in spring in a nursery bed; divide roots in autumn.

Care: Mulch with well-decayed manure or compost in spring. Removing the flowers as they appear improves root size and quality.

Recommended: Basic species.

Related plants: *I. conyzae*, more aromatic leaves and roots; *I. magnifica*, larger species.

INULA HELENIUM

Robust and impressive when seen against a dark background, and respected since early monastic times as an antiseptic. Cultivated in parts of Europe for its roots, used as a vegetable and in perfumery, and also crystallized as confectionery.

39

Iris Orris (Root), Florentine Iris

IRIS 'FLORENTINA'

A sweetly-scented iris flowering in early summer, the inspiration for the heraldic fleur-de-lys and widely cultivated in Mediterranean regions for its fragrant violet-scented root, used in perfumes and liqueurs. (syn. *Iris germanica* var. *florentina*.)

Plant type:	Hardy rhizomatous perennial.
Season of use:	Dig roots at any time for drying.
Height:	90cm (3ft)
Spread:	30cm (12in)
Soil:	Deep, rich and very well-drained.
Positioning:	Full sun, 30cm (12in) apart.
Planting time:	Just after flowering best; alternatively autumn or spring.
Propagation:	Divide roots, taking pieces of young rhizomes, each with a growing tip.
Care:	Plant rhizomes near the surface and keep weed-free. Resists drought well, but occasional watering and a spring feed improves rhizome quality. Cut back faded flower stems, and shorten foliage in autumn.
Recommended:	Basic variety only.
Related plants:	*I. foetidissima* (Gladwyn, Stinking Iris), greyish purple flowers, bright orange seeds; *I. versicolor* (Blue Flag), blue, sometimes red.

Laurus nobilis (Sweet) Bay, Bay Laurel

Plant type: Moderately hardy evergreen shrub or tree.

Season of use: Pick leaves at any time, to use fresh or dried; pick ripe berries in autumn to press for oil.

Height: Up to 15m (48ft), more usually 3m (10ft)

Spread: 2–9m (6–28ft)

Soil: Rich and well-drained.

Positioning: Full sun or light shade with shelter from frosts and cold winds.

Planting time: Early autumn or spring.

Propagation: Take semi-ripe cuttings in summer in a cold frame; layer branches in autumn.

Care: Mulch in autumn and feed in spring. Prune to shape in summer. Protect plants, especially young ones, in cold winters.

Recommended: Basic species; also golden form 'Aurea'.

Related plants: *Umbellularia californica* (Californian Laurel), more aromatic foliage.

LAURUS NOBILIS

The best shrubby herb for a prominent position in herb gardens or ornamental containers, and often clipped into topiary shapes. The leaves have culinary and medicinal uses, while an oil from the berries is used in perfumery.

Lavandula angustifolia English Lavender

LAVANDULA ANGUSTIFOLIA 'HIDCOTE'

A herb collection without lavender would be unthinkable. All kinds are attractive throughout the year, but especially when covered with fragrant flowers eagerly visited by bees. Essential for perfume, pot-pourri and aromatherapy.

Plant type: Hardy perennial evergreen shrub.

Season of use: Pick flowers just before fully opened in mid-summer, and dry slowly; pick flowering shoots and leaves mid-summer for distillation.

Height: 45cm–1m (18in–3ft)

Spread: 30–75cm (12–30in)

Soil: Ordinary, light and very free-draining.

Positioning: Full sun, 30cm (12in) apart.

Planting time: Spring or autumn.

Propagation: Take semi-ripe cuttings in late summer or autumn; divide plants or layer branches in autumn.

Care: Mulch in autumn and feed in spring with rose fertilizer. Trim lightly after flowering, and prune to shape in spring, but avoid cutting into old wood.

Recommended: Other forms include 'Alba' (white), 'Loddon Pink' (tall), 'Munstead' (lax habit).

Related plants: L. × intermedia, especially 'Grappen-hall' and 'Twickel Purple'; L. latifolia (Broad-leaved Lavender); L. stoechas (French Lavender).

Levisticum officinale Lovage

Plant type: Hardy herbaceous perennial.

Season of use: Pick young leaves in spring and summer to use fresh for flavouring; cut hollow main stems before flowering; dig roots in autumn for drying; collect seeds in autumn.

Height: 2m (6ft)

Spread: 75cm (30in)

Soil: Deep, rich and moist but not waterlogged.

Positioning: Cool shade best, but will tolerate full sun.

Planting time: Autumn or spring.

Propagation: Sow in spring outdoors or under glass; divide plants in autumn or spring.

Care: Mulch in autumn and spring, and feed each spring. In mid-summer cut back stems and water well to encourage further young growth.

Recommended: Basic species only.

Related plants: L. chinensis, slightly smaller species; Ligusticum scoticum (Scot's Lovage), milder flavour.

LEVISTICUM OFFICINALE

Lush plants with a powerful celery flavour. Almost all parts can be used, the hollow young stems peeled and sliced like pieces of celery, and the roots dried and powdered as a condiment. The flavour becomes stronger as the season advances.

MALVA MOSCHATA

Several different mallows all have similar medicinal and culinary properties, but this is particularly ornamental with a pronounced musky perfume. Plants flower for a long period in summer, the large blooms contrasting with the finely divided foliage.

Plant type:	Hardy herbaceous perennial.
Season of use:	Pick young leaves to use fresh in spring and early summer; pick flowers in mid-summer for herbal teas.
Height:	90cm (3ft)
Spread:	60cm (2ft)
Soil:	Free-draining and fertile.
Positioning:	Full sun or light shade, 60cm (2ft) apart.
Planting time:	Spring or autumn.
Propagation:	Sow in autumn or late spring, in situ or in pots in a cold frame.
Care:	Mulch in autumn and feed in spring. Water occasionally in very dry weather, and support growth in exposed areas with twiggy sticks.
Recommended:	Basic pink-flowered species; also white 'Alba'.
Related plants:	*M. neglecta* (Dwarf Mallow), almost prostrate, with blue, pink or white flowers; *M. sylvestris* (Common Mallow), taller with violet-pink flowers and many forms.

Melilotus officinalis   Common Melilot, Ribbed Melilot

Plant type: Hardy biennial.

Season of use: Harvest leaves and shoots of flowering plants in the second summer, to use fresh or dried; dry seedheads slowly for flavouring.

Height: 75cm (30in)

Spread: 45cm (18in)

Soil: Light, fertile and well-drained.

Positioning: Full sun or light shade, 30cm (12in) apart.

Planting time: Spring.

Propagation: Sow in late spring in situ, or in pots in a cold frame.

Care: Undemanding. Water in dry weather and support with twiggy sticks in windy situations.

Recommended: Basic species.

Related plants: *M. albus* (White Melilot), taller with fragrant white flowers.

MELILOTUS OFFICINALIS

Once a popular farm crop, with valuable leguminous roots for green manure, this fragrant herb was also a medieval strewing herb and moth repellent. Apart from various medicinal uses, the flowers and seeds are used for flavouring Gruyère cheese.

45

Melissa officinalis Lemon Balm, Bee Balm

MELISSA OFFICINALIS

Welcome for its fresh and invigorating lemon fragrance, particularly popular with bees. Widely used for flavouring and in perfumery, there are many medicinal uses, and the foliage is even used to polish and perfume wooden furniture.

Plant type:	Hardy herbaceous perennial.
Season of use:	Pick fresh young leaves as required; cut whole growing tips just before flowering (late summer) for freezing or drying.
Height:	90cm (3ft)
Spread:	60cm (2ft)
Soil:	Rich and light, moist but not waterlogged.
Positioning:	Full sun or light shade, 30cm (12in) apart.
Planting time:	Autumn or spring.
Propagation:	Sow in spring in situ or in pots under glass; take semi-ripe cuttings in summer; divde plants in autumn or spring.
Care:	Mulch in autumn and feed in spring. Cut back some plants before flowering for a fresh supply of young leaves. Variegated forms produce green seedlings so deadhead after flowering.
Recommended:	Basic species or gold-variegated 'Aurea'.
Related plants:	None.

Mentha × villosa alopecuroides Bowles' Mint

Plant type:	Hardy herbaceous perennial.
Season of use:	Harvest fresh leaves and shoot tips any time during the growing season, just before flowering for freezing or drying, in full flower for distillation.
Height:	90cm (3ft)
Spread:	60cm (2ft) or more
Soil:	Any kind.
Positioning:	Shade or sun, cool in summer.
Planting time:	Spring.
Propagation:	Divide roots in spring; take cuttings of side-shoots and plant in a cold frame in summer.
Care:	Mulch in autumn and feed in spring with a high-potash fertilizer. Cut back some plants just before flowering to rejuvenate growth. Remake beds every 4–5 years.
Recommended:	Only this variety available; M. suaveolens (Apple Mint) sometimes regarded as the same.
Related plants:	M. × gracilis 'Variegata' (Ginger Mint); M. × piperita (Peppermint); M. × p. 'Citrata' (Eau de Cologne Mint).

MENTHA × VILLOSA ALOPECUROIDES

There are many mints and everyone has a favourite. This is one of the best for mint sauce, with a fresh apple scent and larger foliage than some others grown for the same purpose. Like all vigorous mints, best confined to limit its invasiveness.

Monarda didyma Bergamot, Oswego Tea

Plant type:	Hardy herbaceous perennial.
Season of use:	Pick leaves to use fresh any time during growing season; pick leaves and flowers in mid-summer for drying.
Height:	90cm (3ft)
Spread:	30cm (12in)
Soil:	Light, rich and moist.
Positioning:	Full sun or light shade, 23cm (9in) apart.
Planting time:	Autumn or spring.
Propagation:	Sow in spring outdoors or in trays in a cold frame; divide roots in spring.
Care:	Mulch with well-rotted manure in autumn, feed and mulch in spring. Divide and renew mature plants every 2–3 years.
Recommended:	Basic species; also 'Cambridge Scarlet', 'Croftway Pink', 'Snow White'.
Related plants:	M. fistulosa (Wild Bergamot), purple flowers, occasionally white or pink, good on dry soils.

MONARDA DIDYMA

A lovely ornamental herb with an aromatic, almost orangey fragrance. The flowers are spectacular and long-lasting from mid-summer onwards. It has a wide range of herbal uses, especially in the relaxing Oswego tea.

Plant type: Hardy herbaceous perennial.

Season of use: Pick leaves to use fresh from late spring onwards; collect seeds green and immature or ripe and dried, mid-summer.

Height: 90cm (3ft)

Spread: 45cm (18in)

Soil: Deep, rich, moist but free-draining.

Positioning: Light shade, but tolerates full sun; growth appears very early so shelter from cold spring winds.

Planting time: Autumn or spring.

Propagation: Sow in autumn in pots or open ground, and expose to frost; divide roots in autumn or spring.

Care: Mulch in autumn and feed in spring; on light soils water generously in dry weather. Cut back after flowering to promote young foliage. Plants often self-seed freely.

Recommended: Basic species.

Related plants: None.

MYRRHIS ODORATA

An attractively fresh ferny herb, traditionally grown near the kitchen door, since leaves were regularly picked for sweetening cooked fruit dishes. The whole plant is gently medicinal, while the seeds are ground as a spice in some countries.

Nepeta × faassenii Catmint

NEPETA × FAASSENII

An old-fashioned cottage garden plant, exuding a volatile oil that is an aphrodisiac for cats. Traditionally grown as an aromatic edging to flower borders, plants have a number of medicinal virtues and are also used widely in perfumery. (syn. *N. mussinii*.)

Plant type:	Hardy herbaceous perennial.
Season of use:	Pick leaves to use fresh any time during the season; cut flowering stems in summer to use fresh or dry in shade.
Height:	60cm (2ft)
Spread:	38cm (15in)
Soil:	Light or medium, fertile and well-drained.
Positioning:	Full sun, 30cm (12in) apart.
Planting time:	Autumn or spring.
Propagation:	Plant semi-ripe cuttings in a cold frame in summer; divide plants from autumn to spring.
Care:	Mulch in autumn and feed in spring. Trim well back after flowering to encourage young foliage and a second crop of blooms.
Recommended:	Basic species only.
Related plants:	*N. cataria* (Catmint, Catnep), more straggly, loved by cats but less widely available; *N. grandiflora*, tall with long flower spikes.

Ocimum basilicum
Common Basil, Sweet Basil

Plant type: Tender perennial, grown as a half-hardy annual.

Season of use: Pick leaves to use fresh any time during growing season; pick just before flowering for freezing.

Height: 30cm (12in)

Spread: 15cm (6in)

Soil: Rich, moist and free-draining.

Positioning: Full sun with shelter from wind.

Planting time: After the last spring frosts.

Propagation: Sow in warmth under glass, in small pots to avoid root disturbance, or outside in early summer.

Care: Water regularly but avoid wetting foliage. Trim occasionally to prevent flowering and to keep plants neat.

Recommended: Normal species; also cultivated forms 'Fino Verde', 'Lettuce-leaved', 'Napolitano', 'Purple-leaved', 'Ruffles'; 'O. b. var. citriodorum (Lemon Basil), spreading, grey-green; O. b var. minimum (Bush Basil), tiny leaves, strong flavour.

Related plants: O. sanctum (Holy Basil), larger with pink flowers.

OCIMUM BASILICUM

The most popular annual herb for adding Mediterranean warmth and spicy richness to summer salads; used since early Egyptian times for culinary and medicinal purposes, and also distilled for adding to soaps, cosmetics and liqueurs.

Oenothera biennis (Common) Evening Primrose

OENOTHERA BIENNIS

Plant type:	Hardy biennial.
Season of use:	Harvest leaves, shoots and flowers in second year to use fresh; dig roots in autumn, or early spring before growth revives.
Height:	Up to 1.8m (6ft), often less
Spread:	45cm (18in)
Soil:	Light, well-drained and fairly fertile.
Positioning:	Full sun, 30cm (12in) apart.
Planting time:	Autumn.
Propagation:	Sow in situ in late spring or summer, or in a seedbed for transplanting.
Care:	Undemanding. Leave seedheads to ripen as plants self-seed freely.
Recommended:	Basic species only.
Related plants:	*O. glazioviana*, syn. *O. erythrosepala* (Large-flowered Evening Primrose), larger flowers, edible shoots and roots; *O. tetragona*, syn. *O. fruticosa* ssp. *glauca* (Sun-drops), ornamental, flowering during the day.

Evening primrose is an important source of gamma-linoleic oil, but plants are also edible. The roots ('German rampion') are used as a vegetable, and the leaves from dormant rosettes as a winter potherb. Flowers open in the evening, so plant where they catch the setting sun.

Origanum vulgare Oregano, Wild Marjoram

Plant type: Hardy evergreen perennial.

Season of use: Pick leaves at any time to use fresh; pick flowers in late summer; harvest whole plant at flowering time for distillation or drying.

Height: 60cm (2ft)

Spread: 30cm (12in)

Soil: Light, rich and well-drained.

Positioning: Full sun for best flavour, or light shade (gold forms), 30cm (12in) apart.

Planting time: Early autumn or late spring.

Propagation: Sow seeds in spring, in situ or in a nursery bed; take semi-ripe cuttings in late summer; divide plants in spring; layer stems in autumn.

Care: Feed with bonemeal in autumn and a light dressing of general fertilizer in spring. Renew plants every 3–4 years to keep them vigorous.

Recommended: Basic species; also white-flowered var. *album*, golden 'Aureum' and variegated 'Gold Tip'.

Related plants: O. majorana (Knotted Marjoram).

ORIGANUM VULGARE

From a low winter hummock of tight foliage the upright flowering stems erupt in summer to attract bees and hoverflies. Indispensable for a variety of medicinal, cosmetic and culinary uses.

Pelargonium graveolens Rose geranium

PELARGONIUM GRAVEOLENS 'LADY PLYMOUTH'

Best known of a wide range of wonderfully scented pelargoniums and, in its plain form, a commercial source of oil of geranium. The leaves are used for pot-pourri and for flavouring drinks, and in perfume and aromatherapy. Small, pale pink flowers appear in summer and autumn.

Plant type:	Tender perennial.
Season of use:	Pick leaves all year round, to use fresh; pick leaves just before flowering for drying.
Height:	Up to 1.2m (4ft)
Spread:	60–90cm (2–3ft)
Soil:	Rich, free-draining outdoors, or soil-based medium for pots.
Positioning:	Foliage plant indoors; full sun outside in frost-free gardens or as summer bedding 60cm (2ft) apart.
Planting time:	After last spring frosts.
Propagation:	Sow indoors in spring; root cuttings of side-shoots in late summer under glass.
Care:	Prune to shape in spring and grow in a sunny place; stand outside in summer for compact growth. Plants grown permanently outdoors are cut down in autumn and mulched with leaves or straw.
Recommended:	Only 'Lady Plymouth'.
Related plants:	Popular kinds include *P. crispum* (lemon), *P.* Fragrans Group (nutmeg), *P. odoratissimum* (apple) and *P. tomentosum* (mint).

Petroselinum crispum Parsley

Plant type: Hardy biennial.

Season of use: Can be harvested all year round with winter protection.

Height: 15–30cm (6–12in)

Spread: 15–20cm (6–8in)

Soil: Rich, moist and well-drained, slightly alkaline.

Positioning: Full sun or light shade, 15cm (6in) apart.

Planting time: Spring, and again in summer.

Propagation: Sow in early spring and again in early summer for succession, in drills outdoors or under glass (germination is often slow); plants self-seed freely.

Care: Water regularly in dry weather and remove flower stems unless seeds are needed. Pot for winter use or cover with cloches.

Recommended: Many other good varieties, such as 'Champion Moss Curled' and 'Curlina'.

Related plants: Tall plain-leafed or 'Italian' parsley, var. *neapolitanum*, has a stronger flavour, and tolerates extremes of cold and drought.

PETROSELINUM CRISPUM 'BRAVOUR'

This ancient herb was mentioned by Homer, and remains an essential kitchen garden plant. It is a popular garnish, *fine herbe* and digestive stimulant, while the leaves, roots and seeds are used medicinally under supervision.

Portulaca oleracea var. sativa (Summer) Purslane

PORTULACA OLERACEA VAR. SATIVA

Usually grown as a cultivated form of the true species, taller with larger leaves and a mild flavour. Although mainly eaten as a cooked vegetable, leaves are edible raw and may be pickled for winter use. The golden forms make attractive ground cover.

Plant type: Slightly tender annual.

Season of use: Harvest leaves and stems before flowering, mid- to late summer, to use fresh.

Height: 30cm (12in)

Spread: 30cm (12in)

Soil: Light, fertile and well-drained.

Positioning: Full sun or light shade.

Planting time: Always sown in situ in spring and summer and cannot be transplanted.

Propagation: Sow in mid-spring, and again every 4–6 weeks until late summer for continuity.

Care: Thin to 23cm (9in) apart each way. Water in dry weather. Cut shoot tips or whole plants as soon as large enough – 3–4 cuts should be possible before plants are exhausted.

Recommended: Green forms listed as 'Common', 'Green' or 'Kitchen'; and also golden forms.

Related plants: *P. oleracea* (Wild Purslane), smaller, with narrow leaves and a sharper flavour.

Pulmonaria officinalis <small>Lungwort, Mary and Joseph</small>

Plant type: Hardy herbaceous perennial.

Season of use: Harvest young leaves in spring and summer to use fresh; harvest whole flowering plant in spring, to use fresh or dried; dig roots in winter for drying.

Height: 30cm (12in)

Spread: 45cm (18in)

Soil: Light, fairly rich and moisture retentive.

Positioning: Light or semi-shade, 38cm (15in) apart.

Planting time: Spring or autumn.

Propagation: Seeds (species only) sown outdoors in spring; divide roots in autumn or just after flowering.

Care: Water well in dry seasons. Deadhead after flowering, mulch in autumn and feed in spring. Divide and replant every 4–5 years.

Recommended: Basic species; also 'Blue Mist', 'Cambridge Blue' and 'Sissinghurst White'.

Related plants: P. rubra, red flowers mid-winter onwards; P. saccharata, syn. P. 'Picta' (Bethlehem Sage), larger, heavily spotted leaves, lilac, white or blue flowers.

PULMONARIA OFFICINALIS

A valuable early-flowering herb, this is one of the best ground cover plants for shady spots. It is renowned for its medicinal uses: the roots and top growth are used to treat bronchial disorders, while young leaves are a spring potherb traditionally added to soups and stews.

Rosa gallica var. officinalis (The) Apothecaries' Rose

ROSA GALLICA VAR. OFFICINALIS

This is one of the oldest roses and a parent of many modern kinds. The rich and penetrating fragrance of its blooms makes up for the short flowering season, and can be distilled for medicines, cosmetics and preserves

Plant type:	Hardy shrub.
Season of use:	Pick flowers in early summer.
Height:	1.2m (4ft)
Spread:	90cm–1.2m (3–4ft)
Soil:	Fairly heavy, fertile and well-drained.
Positioning:	Full sun.
Planting time:	Autumn.
Propagation:	Plant hardwood cuttings in sheltered ground in late autumn.
Care:	Mulch well with well-rotted manure in autumn or spring, and dress in spring and summer with rose fertilizer. Prune in spring to remove damaged or overcrowded shoots, plus one or two of the oldest stems each year.
Recommended:	Basic species; also pink and white striped sport 'Rosa Mundi' (*R. g.* 'Versicolor', syn. *R. versicolor*).
Related plants:	*R. × alba* 'Alba Semiplena' (White Rose of York), tall and fragrant; *R. centifolia* (Cabbage Rose) and *R. damascena* (Damask Rose), both used to distil attar of roses; *R. rugosa* (Japanese Rose), with decorative hips.

Plant type: Hardy or half-hardy evergreen shrub.

Season of use: Cut shoot tips any time for flavouring and for teas; cut shoots at flowering time to use fresh, or dry in shade.

Height: 45cm–4m (18in–13ft)

Spread: 45cm–1.8m (18in–6ft)

Soil: Light, fairly fertile and very free-draining.

Positioning: Full sun with shelter from cold winds.

Planting time: Spring or autumn.

Propagation: Sow seeds (species only) under glass in spring; plant semi-ripe cuttings in summer in a cold frame; layer branches in autumn.

Care: Mulch in autumn and feed with a rose fertilizer in spring. Clip in late spring, or trim to shape after flowering and cut out a few of the oldest branches. Some forms need shelter in cold winters.

Recommended: Many other cultivars including 'Benenden Blue', 'Majorca Pink', 'Miss Jessop's Upright', 'Prostratus', syn. R. repens (low-growing), 'Severn Sea' (bright blue).

Related plants: None.

ROSMARINUS OFFICINALIS 'TUSCAN BLUE'

Wet washing was once spread out on rosemary hedges because of their intense fragrance. 'Tuscan Blue', above, is a particularly decorative form. There are tall upright kinds and tumbling prostrate forms, all desirable but some not very hardy, so choose carefully. 'Tuscan Blue' (above) is a particularly decorative form.

Rumex scutatus French Sorrel, Buckler-leaf Sorrel

RUMEX SCUTATUS

This is the most decorative sorrel to grow for soups, teas and medicinal purposes; the roots are also used as a tonic. The sharply flavoured leaves were once made into a stain remover, 'salts of sorrel', and contain oxalic acid, so consume sparingly.

Plant type: Hardy herbaceous perennial.

Season of use: Pick young leaves and buds before flowering in summer, to use fresh or freeze; dig roots in summer to use fresh.

Height: 30cm (12in)

Spread: 1.2m (4ft)

Soil: Rich and fairly moist; avoid very heavy, wet ground.

Positioning: Full sun or light shade, 60cm (24in) apart.

Planting time: Spring or autumn.

Propagation: Sow in spring, outdoors or in trays in a cold frame; divide roots in spring.

Care: Undemanding. Water in very dry weather, and feed lightly in spring. Gather leaves frequently and remove flower stems to prolong cropping. Divide and replant every few years.

Recommended: Basic species; also decorative 'Silver Shield'.

Related plants: *R. acetosa* (Sorrel), coarse plant with large dock-like leaves; *R. patientia* (Herb Patience), tall, large leaves used as spinach.

Ruta graveolens Rue, Herb of Grace

Plant type: Hardy evergreen shrub.

Season of use: Pick leaves from flowering plant, to use fresh, or dry in shade.

Height: 75cm (30in)

Spread: 45cm (18in)

Soil: Rich and well-drained, with a little lime.

Positioning: Full sun, 20cm (8in) apart for low hedges.

Planting time: Spring.

Propagation: Sow seeds (species and 'Harlequin' only) outdoors in spring; plant semi-ripe cuttings in late summer in a cold frame.

Care: Mulch in autumn and feed in spring. As some die-back may occur in cold winters, wait until late spring and then cut plants back by half or closely trim hedges. The flowers are insignificant and may be removed.

Recommended: Basic species; also variegated 'Harlequin' and 'Variegata'.

Related plants: None.

RUTA GRAVEOLENS 'JACKMAN'S BLUE'

This rich steely-blue cultivar is the best form of pungent rue, used since the sixteenth century for medicinal purposes. Its essential oil flavours many foods and drinks, but allergic reactions are common, so treat the plant with caution.

Salvia officinalis (Common) Sage

SALVIA OFFICINALIS

One of the essential culinary herbs for stuffings and flavourings. There are a number of very variable forms, all worth growing although the prettiest are often less hardy. Cultivated for centuries for its antiseptic essential oil and tonic properties.

Plant type:	Hardy evergreen shrub.
Season of use:	Pick leaves and tips at any time to use fresh; pick just before flowering to dry in shade.
Height:	60cm (24in)
Spread:	75cm (30in)
Soil:	Light, fairly fertile and free-draining.
Positioning:	Full sun, coloured forms with shelter from winds.
Planting time:	Spring.
Propagation:	Sow seeds (species only) in spring under glass; take semi-ripe cuttings in summer; layer stems in autumn.
Care:	Mulch in autumn and feed in spring. Trim just as flower spikes appear, but leave some plants to bloom for ornament. Renew every 3–4 years.
Recommended:	Plain narrow-leafed and broad-leafed forms; 'Icterina' (two-toned green), 'Purpurascens' and 'Tricolor' (white, pink and green).
Related plants:	S. sclarea (Clary Sage), basis of muscatel oil; S. fruticosa, syn. S. triloba (Three-lobed Sage), large, used for sage tea.

Salvia sclarea Clary (Sage), Muscatel Sage

Plant type: Hardy evergreen herbaceous biennial (or short-lived perennial).

Season of use: Pick fresh leaves at any time, or just before flowering for drying in shade; gather and dry seeds in autumn.

Height: 60–90cm (2–3ft)

Spread: 30–45cm (12–18in)

Soil: Light, dryish and free-draining

Positioning: Full sun, 20–30cm (8–12in) apart in groups.

Planting time: Transplant in spring.

Propagation: Sow seeds in autumn or mid-spring, in situ or under glass for pricking out into small pots.

Care: Plants for herbal use are best sown in rows and harvested all together in summer. Plants often self-seed freely.

Recommended: Basic species; also 'Turkestanica', a selected form with larger flowers lasting until autumn.

Related plants: *S. viridis*, syn. *S. horminum* (Clary), ornamental annual or biennial with many varieties.

SALVIA SCLAREA

A decorative plant, often confused with the closely related annual Clary grown as summer bedding. Clary Sage is also known as Muscatel Sage, because it is the commercial source of the Muscatel oil used in perfumery. Its seeds and leaves also have medicinal value.

63

Sambucus nigra Elderberry, Common Elder, European Elder

SAMBUCUS NIGRA 'MARGINATA'

An essential shrub, once credited with strong magical powers as the guardian of all herbs. Every part can be used, for drinks, jams and preserves, for dyes and cosmetics, or for various medicinal purposes. Variegated forms are highly attractive shrubs in the flower garden.

Plant type:	Hardy deciduous shrub or small tree.
Season of use:	Pick fresh leaves, buds and flowers in summer, berries in autumn; harvest roots and stem pith in winter.
Height:	Up to 10m (36ft)
Spread:	5–6m (16–20ft)
Soil:	Any soil.
Positioning:	Full sun or light shade, as a specimen shrub or tree in herb, flower and wild gardens.
Planting time:	Autumn or spring.
Propagation:	Take suckers or hardwood cuttings in autumn; sow seeds (species only) in autumn.
Care:	Undemanding. Prune to shape in winter, and cut down ornamentals every year to stimulate young growth.
Recommended:	Basic species; 'Aurea' (gold leaves), 'Guincho Purple' (rich red leaves), 'Laciniata' (cut-leafed).
Related plants:	*S. canadensis* (American Elder), similar uses; *S. racemosa* (European Red Elder), scarlet berries, decorative forms.

Sanguisorba minor   Salad Burnet

Plant type: Hardy herbaceous or semi-shrubby perennial.

Season of use: Pick young leaves spring and summer to use fresh, or pick just before flowering for drying; dig roots in spring and dry.

Height: 60cm (24in)

Spread: 25cm (10in)

Soil: Light, fertile and free-draining, with lime.

Positioning: Full sun or light shade, 20cm (8in) apart.

Planting time: Spring or early summer.

Propagation: Sow seeds in late spring in a cold frame; divide roots in spring.

Care: Feed in spring. Remove flowers to extend useful season. Plants self-seed freely if allowed.

Recommended: Basic species only.

Related plants: *S. officinalis* (Great Burnet), taller plant for moist ground, blood-red flowers.

SANGUISORBA MINOR

A pretty little plant maturing into a neat tussock of leaves that taste of fresh cucumber and may be used in summer drinks and salads. It has various medicinal uses, while the roots produce a black dye and were once used in tanning leather. (syn. *Poterium sanguisorba*)

Santolina chamaecyparissus Lavender Cotton

SANTOLINA CHAMAECYPARISSUS

Pungent Mediterranean shrub introduced by the early Tudors as a hedging plant for parterres and knot gardens, but used since classical Greek times as a moth repellent and known in France as 'Garde Robe' for this reason. (syn. *S. incana*)

Plant type:	Hardy evergreen perennial shrub.
Season of use:	Pick leaves before flowering, dry and strip from stalks; pick flowers in mid-summer for drying.
Height:	45cm (18in)
Spread:	60cm (24in)
Soil:	Light, fairly fertile and free draining.
Positioning:	Full sun with shelter from cold winter winds, 45cm (18in) apart.
Planting time:	Mid- to late spring.
Propagation:	Take semi-ripe cuttings with a heel in summer and plant in a cold frame; layer stems in autumn.
Care:	Mulch in autumn and feed lightly in spring. Clip to shape after last spring frosts; trim just before flowering and again in late summer
Recommended:	Basic species and 'Lambrook Silver'; also dwarf 'Lemon Queen' and var. *nana*.
Related plants:	*S. pinnata* ssp. *neapolitana* (Italian Lavender), silvery grey leaves; *S. rosmarinifolia*, syn. *S. virens*, yellow flowers, especially in ssp. *rosmarinifolia*.

Plant type:	Hardy evergreen shrub.
Season of use:	Pick leaves all year round to use fresh, or just before flowering for drying or distilling.
Height:	38cm (15in)
Spread:	30cm (12in)
Soil:	Light, fairly fertile, dry or free-draining.
Positioning:	Full sun with shelter from cold winds, especially on moist soils, 30cm (12in) apart.
Planting time:	Late spring or autumn.
Propagation:	Sow in spring under cool glass; plant semi-ripe cuttings in summer in a cold frame.
Care:	Mulch in autumn, and feed lightly in spring. Trim to shape in late spring to allow for frost damage.
Recommended:	Basic species; also 'Prostrate White' and 'Purple Mountain'.
Related plants:	S. hortensis (Summer Savory), short annual with intense flavour; S. spicigera, syn. S. repanda (Creeping Savory), tiny prostrate plant with white flowers.

SATUREJA MONTANA

Of the two familiar savories, with almost similar flavours, this species is the more useful as it is available all year round. Its spicy leaves have been used since Roman times for flavouring, and it is grown commercially for its essential oil.

Smyrnium olusatrum Alexanders

SMYRNIUM OLUSATRUM

Plant type:	Hardy biennial or short-lived perennial.
Season of use:	Pick young leaves in spring and summer to use fresh; blanch young shoots in the second spring; gather seeds in late summer; dig roots in winter.
Height:	1.2m (4ft)
Spread:	60cm (2ft)
Soil:	Rich and moist, but not waterlogged.
Positioning:	Full sun or light shade, 45cm (18in) apart.
Planting time:	Late spring or autumn.
Propagation:	Sow in a cold frame, in spring for leaf crops or in late summer for overwintering.
Care:	Mulch in autumn and feed in spring. Cut down top growth in autumn.
Recommended:	Basic species only.
Related plants:	*S. perfoliatum* (Perfoliate Alexanders), taller perennial with interesting yellow-green flowers favoured by flower arrangers.

Widely grown as a potherb, to be added to soups and stews, until the eighteenth century. Now, it is grown as an important condiment and medicinal plant. All parts may be used, including the roots and blanched shoots as vegetables, and the seeds as a pepper substitute.

Stachys officinalis (Wood) Betony, Bishop's Wort

STACHYS OFFICINALIS

Plant type:	Hardy herbaceous perennial.
Season of use:	Harvest leaves and stems before flowering in summer, to use fresh or for drying.
Height:	60–90cm (2–3ft)
Spread:	45cm (18in)
Soil:	Most kinds.
Positioning:	Full sun or semi-shade, 30cm (12in) apart.
Planting time:	Autumn or spring.
Propagation:	Sow seeds (species only) in situ in late summer or in trays under glass in late spring; divide roots in autumn or spring.
Care:	Undemanding. Mulch in autumn after cutting down all top growth, and feed in spring.
Recommended:	Basic species; also 'Alba' (white) and 'Rosea Superba' (double pink).
Related plants:	S. affinis (Chinese Artichoke), small conical ringed tubers; S. byzantina, syn. S. lanata (Lamb's Ears, Lamb's Tongue), foliage ground cover, best as non-flowering 'Silver Carpet'; S. macrantha, large rosy-violet flowers.

A simple woodland plant with a long medicinal pedigree; 'of great esteem among the ancients' according to one classical writer, but now used only as an ornamental herb and ingredient of herbal tobaccos. A fine ground cover plant for shady corners. (syn. S. betonica)

Symphytum officinale Comfrey, Knitbone

SYMPHYTUM OFFICINALE

A stout woodland plant with leaves and roots renowned for their medicinal properties (although it is not now recommended for internal use), and a favourite with organic gardeners who grow it for making compost and liquid feeds.

Plant type:	Hardy herbaceous perennial.
Season of use:	Pick leaves during growing season, to use fresh, wilted or dried; dig roots in winter to use fresh or dried.
Height:	1.2m (4ft)
Spread:	60cm (2ft)
Soil:	Moist and fairly rich.
Positioning:	Full sun or light shade, 45cm (18in) apart.
Planting time:	Autumn or late spring.
Propagation:	Take cuttings in spring; divide roots in autumn.
Care:	Water in dry weather and mulch in autumn with decayed manure. Feed in spring and again at mid-summer if heavily cropped.
Recommended:	Basic species, or decorative var. *coccineum* (crimson flowers).
Related plants:	*S. caucasicum* (Caucasian Comfrey), bright blue flowers; *S. ibiricum*, syn. *S. grandiflorum* (Creeping Comfrey), drought-resistant ground cover, cream/orange flowers; *S. × uplandicum* (Russian Comfrey), lush vigorous hybrid for leaf production.

Tanacetum parthenium Feverfew, Nosebleed

Plant type: Hardy herbaceous perennial.

Season of use: Pick leaves to use fresh at any time; harvest whole green plant just before flowering and dry in shade.

Height: 60cm (24in)

Spread: 30cm (12in)

Soil: Light and fairly fertile, dryish or well-drained.

Positioning: Full sun.

Planting time: Spring.

Propagation: Sow seeds (species and 'Aureum' only) on the surface in spring, outdoors or in trays; plant semi-ripe cuttings in a cold frame in summer.

Care: Undemanding. Mulch in autumn and feed in spring.

Recommended: Basic species; also golden 'Aureum', double 'Plenum', 'Ball's Double White' and 'White Bonnet'.

Related plants: *T. balsamita* (Alecost), spicy leaves used for flavouring; *T. cinerariifolium* (Pyrethrum), used as an insecticide; *T. vulgare* (Tansy), camphor fragrance.

TANACETUM PARTHENIUM

A bitter medicinal herb, currently popular as a migraine treatment. With its delicate ferny leaves it is also exceptionally ornamental, especially in its golden and double-flowered forms. Once established it self-seeds freely in unexpected places. (syn. *Matricaria parthenium*.)

Teucrium chamaedrys Wall Germander

TEUCRIUM CHAMAEDRYS

The ancient Greeks named this plant, once a popular digestive and medicinal herb, and still important in the preparation of wines and liqueurs. One of the handful of dense evergreen herbs that tolerate formal clipping and widely used for parterre or knot garden hedges

Plant type:	Hardy evergreen sub-shrub.
Season of use:	Use fresh leaves any time for herbal teas; dry whole plants just before flowering for medicinal use.
Height:	30–50cm (12–20in)
Spread:	20–30cm (8–12in)
Soil:	Ordinary and well-drained, with a little lime.
Positioning:	Full sun, 15cm (6in) apart in small groups, or as edging and dwarf hedges.
Planting time:	Autumn or spring.
Propagation:	Sow seeds under glass in spring; take semi-ripe cuttings under glass in summer; divide plants in autumn.
Care:	Undemanding. In spring mulch and feed with a general fertilizer. Trim to shape in early spring, formal hedges again in summer.
Recommended:	Basic species; 'Nanum' is a dwarf carpeting herb; leaves of 'Variegatum' have cream markings.
Related plants:	*T. fruticans* (Shrubby Germander) is larger, up to 2.4m (8ft) high, with lilac, white or dark blue flowers.

Thymus vulgaris Wild Thyme

Plant type: Hardy evergreen perennial shrub.

Season of use: Pick leaves to use fresh at any time; pick flowering tips to use fresh, or dry in the sun.

Height: 30cm (18in)

Spread: 30–45cm (12–18in)

Soil: Light, fairly fertile and very well-drained, with a little lime.

Positioning: Full sun, 30cm (12in) apart.

Planting time: Spring or autumn.

Propagation: Sow seeds (species only) in spring, outdoors or in trays under glass; divide plants in spring; plant semi-ripe cuttings in a cold frame in late summer; layer branches in autumn.

Care: Mulch lightly in autumn and feed in spring. Clip to shape after flowering and again in autumn, and renew every 2–3 years.

Recommended: Normal species for flavour, or 'Silver Posie'.

Related plants: *T. × citriodorus* (Lemon Thyme), strongly flavoured, best as 'Aureus' or 'Silver Queen'; *T. mastichina*, Spanish, pink flowers.

THYMUS VULGARIS

There are literally hundreds of species and cultivars of thyme, so popular is this essential herb. Wild thyme is a tough woody plant, slightly straggly, but with exceptional flavour; for decorative use choose a variegated form.

Trigonella foenum-graecum Fenugreek

TRIGONELLA FOENUM-GRAECUM

One of the oldest culinary plants, with sweet-scented flowers in summer and sickle-shaped pods of aromatic seeds used as a condiment and for sprouting. Young green shoots can be added to salads, while the whole green plant is cooked like spinach.

Plant type: Half-hardy annual.

Season of use: Pick leaves to use fresh during growth; harvest whole green plant to use fresh before seeds are mature; collect ripe seeds in autumn.

Height: 60cm (24in)

Spread: 10cm (4in)

Soil: Light, fairly fertile, well-drained and alkaline.

Positioning: Full sun, in rows 20cm (8in) apart.

Planting time: Always sown in situ, and cannot be transplanted.

Propagation: Sow in mid-spring, barely covering with soil.

Care: Thin to 15cm (6in) apart, and in dry weather water during early growth. Pull up plants when seedpods are nearly ripe and hang in bundles to dry.

Recommended: Basic species only.

Related plants: *T. caerulea* (Blue Melilot, Sweet Trefoil), blue-flowered species.

Tropaeolum majus Nasturtium

Plant type: Tender perennial, grown as a hardy annual.

Season of use: Pick leaves spring and summer to use fresh; pick flowers in summer; collect seeds while green, or when ripe for seasoning.

Height: Tall 3m (10ft), dwarf 25–38cm (10–15in)

Spread: Tall 2m (6ft), dwarf 45cm (18in)

Soil: Rich and moist for best leaf crops, dry and impoverished for flowers.

Positioning: Full sun with shelter from winds, 20cm (8in) apart.

Planting time: After spring frosts.

Propagation: Sow spring or early summer in situ, or in pots under glass.

Care: Water young plants and those grown as leaf crops. Check for aphids and caterpillars.

Recommended: 'Tall Mixed'; also dwarf 'Double Gleam Mixed', 'Dwarf Compact Mixed', 'Empress of India' (crimson) and 'Tom Thumb Mixed'.

Related plants: *T. peregrinum* (Canary Creeper), hardy annual climber.

TROPAEOLUM MAJUS

Strikingly beautiful and easily grown plants, not just for the glorious rich colours of their edible flowers but also for the leaves, traditionally used in summer salads and sandwiches. Both flower buds and seeds are pungently hot and may be pickled.

75

Tussilago farfara Coltsfoot, Coughwort

TUSSILAGO FARFARA

A remarkable wild plant that produces clusters of bright yellow flowers very early in spring, followed by shapely woolly leaves. All parts of the plant are useful: the flowers for wine, leaves for medicinal purposes and the roots boiled to make coltsfoot rock (candy).

Plant type:	Hardy herbaceous perennial.
Season of use:	Pick flowers before fully open in early spring, to use fresh or for drying; pick leaves in summer, to use fresh or dried; dig roots in winter and boil to make sweets.
Height:	45cm (18in)
Spread:	45cm (18in)
Soil:	Most moist soils.
Positioning:	Full sun or light shade, 30cm (12in) apart.
Planting time:	Autumn or late spring.
Propagation:	Sow in situ in summer, or in pots in a cold frame in late spring; divide roots in autumn; take root cuttings in late winter.
Care:	Undemanding. Do not feed or mulch; hoe or pull up unwanted seedlings, and divide expanding colonies every few years.
Recommended:	Basic species.
Related plants:	None.

Valeriana officinalis Common Valerian, Garden Heliotrope

Plant type: Hardy herbaceous perennial.

Season of use: Dig roots in autumn, to use fresh, or dry in the shade.

Height: 1.2m (4ft)

Spread: 60cm (2ft)

Soil: Rich and moist.

Positioning: Full sun or deep shade, 45cm (18in) apart.

Planting time: Autumn.

Propagation: Sow in spring in situ, or in a cold frame; divide roots in autumn.

Care: Water in dry weather on poorer soils. Mulch with compost or well-rotted manure in autumn, and feed in spring. Dig roots after leaf fall from plants at least 2 years old.

Recommended: Basic species or cream speckled 'Variegata'.

Related plants: *V. celtica* (Nard), prostrate plant with yellow-brown flowers; *V. phu* (Cretan Spikenard), white-flowered, with gold ('Aurea') and deep red ('Purpurea') forms.

VALERIANA OFFICINALIS

A powerful native herb (sometimes called Heal-All), attractive to cats and used for centuries to treat a variety of nervous ailments. The rather brittle roots may also be cooked as a vegetable and used for flavouring, but avoid large quantities.

Verbena officinalis Vervain, Holy Herb

VERBENA OFFICINALIS

An ancient herb, called *Herba sacra* by the Romans, and steeped in folklore and magic. Despite a long medicinal pedigree and its current use in homeopathy, it is a wild and undistinguished plant visually, one for comprehensive collections.

Plant type: Hardy herbaceous perennial.

Season of use: Harvest whole green plant in summer, to use fresh or for drying in the sun.

Height: Up to 90cm (3ft)

Spread: 30cm (12in)

Soil: Rich and moist (but not waterlogged) best; tolerates most fertile soils.

Positioning: Full sun, but tolerates light shade.

Planting time: Autumn.

Propagation: Surface-sow in situ in spring or autumn; divide roots in autumn.

Care: Thin to 30cm (12in) apart, and water well in dry weather. Mulch in autumn and feed in spring. Support the slender branching stems with twiggy sticks.

Recommended: Basic species only.

Related plants: None.

Vinca major (Greater) Periwinkle, Blue Buttons

Plant type:	Hardy evergreen perennial.
Season of use:	Harvest leaves or whole green flowering plant in spring, to use fresh or dried.
Height:	60cm (24in)
Spread:	90cm (3ft)
Soil:	Moist and fertile, with a little lime.
Positioning:	Full sun for best flowers and variegated forms, moderate shade for ground cover.
Planting time:	Spring or autumn.
Propagation:	Divide roots in spring; plant rooted layers at any time; plant semi-ripe cuttings in a cold frame in summer.
Care:	Cut down in spring, and mulch or feed. Trim once or twice if grown as a formal edging.
Recommended:	Basic species; also dark leaved 'Oxyloba' and variegated 'Maculata' and 'Variegata'(syn. 'Elegantissima').
Related plants:	V. minor (Lesser Periwinkle), smaller, with forms 'Alba', 'Argenteovariegata', 'Atropurpurea' (red-flowered) and double blue 'La Grave'.

VINCA MAJOR

A valuable ground cover plant, even in dry shade and on steep banks; flowers appear mainly in spring but also intermittently throughout the year. Used for centuries on cuts to stop bleeding (it is sometimes called 'Cutfinger').

Viola tricolor Wild Pansy, Heartsease

Plant type:	Hardy annual or short-lived perennial.
Season of use:	Harvest whole green flowering plant, spring to autumn, to use fresh or dry in shade.
Height:	20cm (8in)
Spread:	20cm (8in)
Soil:	Light, fairly fertile, dryish or well-drained.
Positioning:	Full sun or light shade, 15cm (6in) apart.
Planting time:	Usually sown in situ, but may be transplanted any time.
Propagation:	Surface-sow outdoors, in spring or summer.
Care:	No special care needed. Cut back leggy plants to induce further flowering and bushy growth.
Recommended:	Basic species only.
Related plants:	*V. odorata* (Sweet Violet), well-known perennial used for its fragrance; *V. sororia* (Sister Violet), North American wild pansy with cultivated forms 'Freckles' and wine-red var. *rubra*.

VIOLA TRICOLOR

Unassuming, almost evergreen and likely to appear anywhere once introduced (an alternative name is 'Johnny Jump-up'); the flowers are variable and prettily marked. Renowned medicinally for heart and blood disorders, and a parent of modern large-flowered pansies.